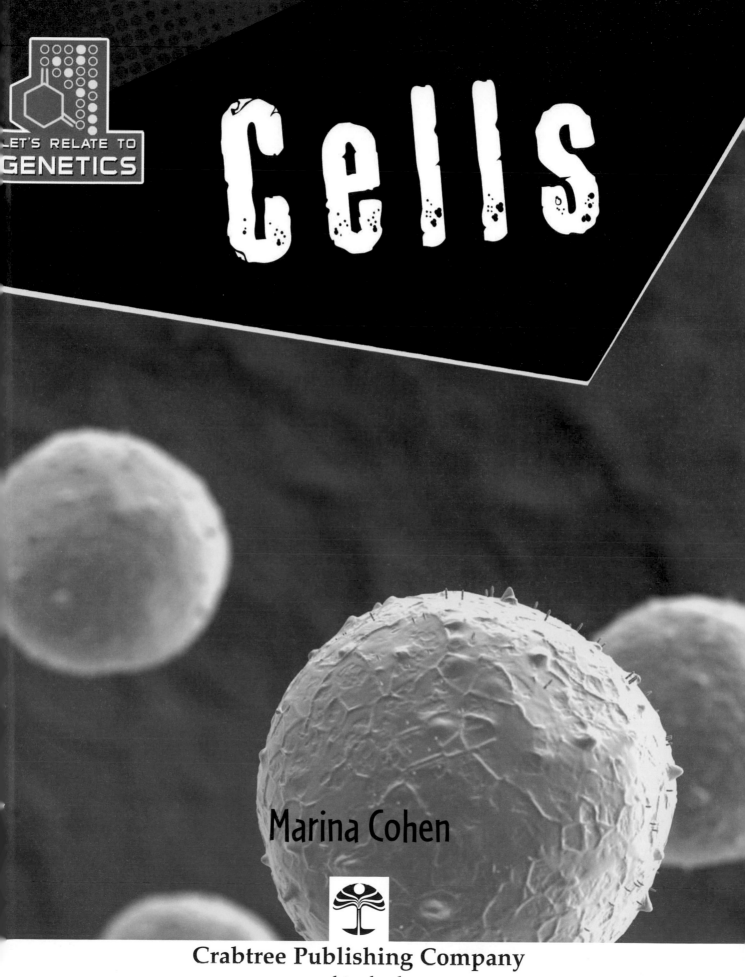

LET'S RELATE TO
GENETICS

Cells

Marina Cohen

Crabtree Publishing Company
www.crabtreebooks.com

Crabtree Publishing Company

www.crabtreebooks.com

Author: Marina Cohen
Coordinating editor: Chester Fisher
Series editor: Jessica Cohn
Editorial director: Kathy Middleton
Editor: Adrianna Morganelli
Proofreader: Reagan Miller
Production coordinator: Katherine Berti
Prepress technician: Katherine Berti
Project manager: Kumar Kunal (Q2AMEDIA)
Art direction: Harleen Mehta (Q2AMEDIA)
Cover design: Tarang Saggar (Q2AMEDIA)
Design: Tarang Saggar (Q2AMEDIA)
Photo research: Mariea Janet (Q2AMEDIA)

Photographs:
123RF: Mark Rasmussen: p. 9 (bottom left), p. 10 (left); Sebastian Kaulitzki: p. 20-21
BigStockPhoto: Alex Merk: p. 5 (bottom left); Kat Sicard: p. 11 (top)
Corbis: Bettmann: p. 6; Mediscan: p. 23 (bottom); Visuals Unlimited: p. 27 (top), 37 (top)
Dreamstime: Frenc: p. 5 (top right), 16; Jack Hollingsworth: p. 8; Oleg Kozlov: p. 24
Fotolia: Fotolia: p. 28; Vanessa: p. 29 (top)
Istockphoto: Panorama: p. 1; Gea Strucks: p. 5 (center right); Keith Webber Jr.: p. 5 (bottom right); Melanie DeFazio: p. 15 (top right); Kimberly Deprey: p. 18; Royce Degrie: p. 19 (top); Peter Garbet: p. 27 (bottom); Mehmet Salih Guler: p. 29 (bottom); Jonathan Heger: p. 32, 33; Henrik Jonsson: p. 25; Panorama: p. 36; Willie B. Thomas: p. 39 (top); Dr. Heinz Linke: p. 41 (bottom left)
Photolibrary: p. 42; P&R Fotos: cover (bottom); Manfred Kage: p. 7 (top); Dr M Yoder: p. 13 (top left); Gopal Murti: p. 14; David Gunn: p. 15 (bottom left); Scott Camazine: p. 17; Laguna Design: p. 19 (bottom); Dennis Kunkel: p. 21 (bottom); Richard Hutchings: p. 38; James Robinson: p. 40
Shutterstock: Sebastian Kaulitzki: cover (top), 23 (top), 26; Karen Givens: p. 4; Shutterstock: p. 5 (center left); Thomas Mounsey: p. 7 (bottom); Ivan Cholakov Gostock: p. 9 (top right); Mariano Heluani: p. 10-11; Kirych: p. 12; Tischenko Irina: p. 13 (top right), 25; Steve Smith: p. 21 (top); Piotr Rzeszutek: p. 22; Marcin Balcerzak: p. 32; Aiti: p. 37 (bottom); Atanas.Dk: p. 39 (bottom); Monika Gniot: p. 41 (top right); Jurgen Ziewe: p. 43 (top left); Darko Kovacevic: p. 43 (top right)
Q2AMedia Art Bank: p. 30-31, 34-35, 44-45

Library and Archives Canada Cataloguing in Publication

Cohen, Marina
　　Cells / Marina Cohen.

(Let's relate to genetics)
Includes index.
ISBN 978-0-7787-4945-5 (bound).--ISBN 978-0-7787-4962-2 (pbk.)

　　1. Cells--Juvenile literature. 2. Cytology--Juvenile literature.
I. Title. II. Series: Let's relate to genetics

QH582.5.C64 2009　　　　j571.6　　　　C2009-903745-9

Library of Congress Cataloging-in-Publication Data

Cohen, Marina.
　　Cells / Marina Cohen.
　　　　p. cm. -- (Let's relate to genetics)
　　Includes index.
　　ISBN 978-0-7787-4945-5 (reinforced lib. bdg. : alk. paper)
　　-- ISBN 978-0-7787-4962-2 (pbk. : alk. paper)
　　1. Cells--Juvenile literature. 2. Cytology--Juvenile literature. I. Title.
　　QH582.5.C64 2010
　　571.6--dc22
　　　　　　　　　　　　　　　　　　　　2009023641

Cover:
Main and inset images:
　　Cells can take in nutrients and get rid of waste. They can join together with each other and communicate. They can move, grow, and reproduce.
How are living things built?:
　　Every living thing on Earth, whether plant or animal, is built with cells. The human body is made up of about 75 trillion cells.

Crabtree Publishing Company
www.crabtreebooks.com　　　1-800-387-7650

Printed in Canada/052011/GF20110411

Published in Canada
Crabtree Publishing
616 Welland Ave.
St. Catharines, Ontario
L2M 5V6

Published in the United States
Crabtree Publishing
PMB 59051
350 Fifth Avenue, 59th Floor
New York, New York 10118

Published in the United Kingdom
Crabtree Publishing
Maritime House
Basin Road North, Hove
BN41 1WR

Published in Australia
Crabtree Publishing
386 Mt. Alexander Rd.
Ascot Vale (Melbourne)
VIC 3032

Contents

What do the Los Angeles Lakers have in common with tulips, jaguars, and sea cucumbers? "Everything" is not a bad answer. They have everything in common because they are all made of cells.

Each living thing on the Earth—from wheat to whales, crickets to cabbage—is made up of cells. These building blocks of life are so small they can only be seen through a microscope. Yet they do some pretty amazing things.

Cells can take in nutrients and get rid of waste. They can join together with each other and communicate. They can move, grow, and reproduce.

The cells in this jaguar's body have instructions for every trait the jaguar has.

Some cells can survive on their own. They are called **unicellular organisms**. Most organisms, however, such as plants, animals, and humans, are **multicellular**. This means they are made up of many cells. In some cases, they are made up of billions, even trillions, of cells. Cells come in all sorts of shapes and sizes. Different kinds of cells are responsible for different jobs.

So what in the world has cells and what does not? In order for something to have cells, it has to have been alive at some point.

Everything around you has **atoms** but not necessarily cells. Atoms are the smallest units of living things and nonliving things. Cells are made of many atoms. Yet cells have something more. Cells contain the essence of life.

In this grouping, the rock and the cell phone do not have cells.

In the Lab

Dust—or is it?
Your body is made up of about 75 trillion cells. Every day you make about 300 billion new cells. Every month, your outer skin cells are completely replaced. Most of that dust on your shelves or under your sofa is made of last month's skin cells.

Chapter 2

A Slice of Life

An ancient Greek philosopher named Democritus decided that all living things were made up of very tiny particles. Yet the real world of cells would remain hidden for another 2,000 years. That's when the microscope was invented.

Zaccharias and Hans Janssen: The first microscopes could magnify objects to only ten times their actual size. They were called *flea glasses*. Zaccharias and Hans Janssen were Dutch eyeglass makers in around 1590. They experimented with different-shaped lenses. Their work led to the creation of the **compound microscope**.

Robert Hooke: In 1665, Robert Hooke magnified a thin slice of cork. He noticed a lot of tiny compartments. He named them *cellulae*, which means "little rooms" in Latin.

The first microscopes all operated using light.

Antonie van Leeuwenhoek: Shortly after Hooke's discovery, Antonie van Leeuwenhoek invented a microscope that could magnify objects up to 270 times their actual size. Leeuwenhoek observed water using an improved microscope. He saw small "things" swimming around. He had discovered **bacteria**. This discovery led to the idea that cells were alive.

Lorenz Oken: In 1805, a German philosopher declared that all living things are made of cells.

Schwann and Schleiden: In 1839, Theodore Schwann and Matthias Schleiden proved that all plants and animals were made up of cells. Cells had common parts. Their observations led Schwann to develop an early form of Cell Theory, principles about what cells are and do.

Rudolf Virchow: In 1858, Rudolf Virchow made a famous statement. He said that cells come from cells that already exist.

The contributions of Hooke, Leeuwenhoek, Oken, Schwann, Schleiden, and Virchow led to today's Cell Theory:

1. All living things are made of one or more cells.
2. The cell is the smallest unit of life.
3. All cells come from other cells that grow and divide.

With a microscope, you can see the bacteria living in water.

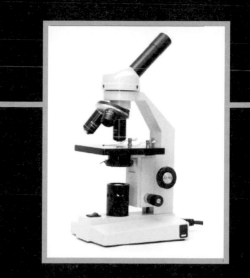

I Spy with My Electron Microscope
Today, electron microscopes can magnify objects by two million times.

Chapter 3

Do you like to chat with friends? Text them? Send them emails? That's very cell-like of you! Cells have an incredible ability to communicate. They can make commands, send encouragement, and make reports.

Instead of words or gestures, cells use chemicals and **molecules**, or clusters of atoms. A cell's sentences are made up of chains of **proteins**. Proteins are molecules needed for an organism to function correctly. It's these conversations that allow trillions of cells to work together as one unit.

To understand what cells say and do, we need to look at cell parts and their functions. First, let's divide cells into two basic categories: the "Slobs" and the "Neat Freaks."

You text with words. Cells "text" using chemicals.

The Slobs

Prokaryotic cells are cells with a large inner space called a **nucleoid**. All cells have genetic material. The genetic material is a kind of code that tells everything about each cell. The genetic material for prokaryotic cells is in one large circular structure and a few smaller circular structures. The structures move freely in the large inner space.

One hundred medium-sized prokaryotic cells lined up would be as thin as a sheet of paper! These tiny cells can live in a wide range of habitats. They survive inside polar ice. They also survive in areas near volcanic vents where temperatures reach 212°F (100°C).

There are two types of prokaryotic cells: bacteria and **archaea**. A bacterium and an archaeon are about the same size and shape. They act differently, however, when processing energy from sunlight or another source.

Prokaryotic Cell

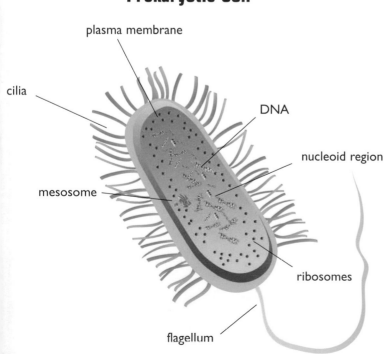

- plasma membrane
- cilia
- DNA
- nucleoid region
- mesosome
- ribosomes
- flagellum

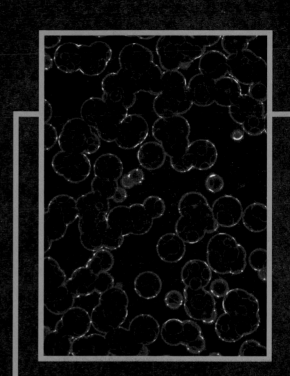

In the Lab

Get 'em Off Me
One hundred thousand bacteria are crawling around on every square centimeter of your skin. In fact, there are more bacteria cells in and on your body than actual human cells. If a nuclear war wiped out civilization, most of Earth's bacteria would not be affected.

Neat Freaks

Eukaryotic cells are in plants and animals, including humans. They are about 10 times as large as prokaryotic cells and can be almost 1,000 times greater in volume. Yet they are not more complex than bacteria and archaea. They are just more organized. Eukaryotic cells keep their genetic material within a neat little compartment called the **nucleus**.

All parts of the cell can be called **organelles**. The word *organelle* means "little organs." They are to the cell as organs are to our bodies.

Eukaryotic Cell

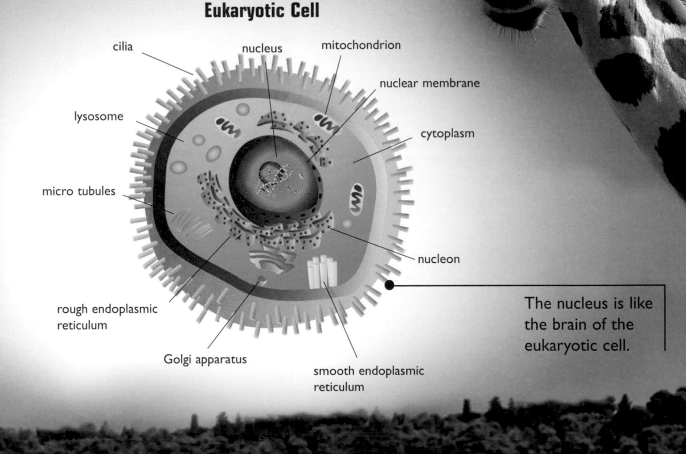

cilia

nucleus

mitochondrion

nuclear membrane

lysosome

cytoplasm

micro tubules

nucleon

rough endoplasmic reticulum

Golgi apparatus

smooth endoplasmic reticulum

The nucleus is like the brain of the eukaryotic cell.

Shape of Things

Cells can look like rods, spheres, or spirals. The rod-shaped cells can be either straight or curved. The spheres can appear oval. Spirals can be thick, thin, or comma-shaped. Some cells have an irregular shape. Some can even change shape as they move. Plant cells usually look like boxes, while skin cells are flat. Nerve cells can appear to have arms, while muscle cells are very thin. A cell's shape is usually linked to its job. For example, thin muscle cells are able to contract so that they can move bones.

The size of a cell can vary greatly as well. If you had 10,000 of a certain bacteria cell, they would still only be as wide as a single strand of hair. The nerve cells in a giraffe's neck are the longest cells. They can be close to ten feet (three meters) in length.

The nerve cells in a giraffe's neck are long. Is that surprising?

Incredible Edible Cells
The largest cells can be seen without a microscope. The yolk of a bird's egg is a single cell. Ostrich egg yolks are the largest known single cells. They are the size of a baseball. One ostrich egg equals about 24 large chicken eggs. You could feed a basketball team and the people on the bench if you scrambled just one of these giant cells.

Cells Inside Out

Everything that a cell needs to survive has to get inside from the outside. Then it needs to travel where it needs to go. If the amount a cell can hold inside becomes too big compared to its surface area, not enough food and chemicals can get inside fast enough. The cell stops growing.

The surface of the cell is like the Great Wall of China. The Great Wall was built to protect the land from invaders. Like the land of China, a cell needs an outer layer that is protective. It needs a wall against invaders.

The exterior layer of the cell is called the **plasma membrane**. Water, oxygen, and carbon dioxide can pass through the plasma membrane freely. Larger material, such as sugar, is more closely regulated.

Cells have walls for protection, much like the Great Wall protected China.

A cell has pores that regulate what goes in and out.

Both prokaryotic cells and eukaryotic plant cells have yet another tough layer outside their cell membranes. That second layer is called a cell wall. Like the plasma membrane, the cell wall protects the cell by not allowing harmful things to pass. The cell wall also has an important job. It provides the cell with its structure. This strong wall can be divided into two parts. These are the primary wall and the secondary wall. The secondary wall forms only after the cell has stopped growing.

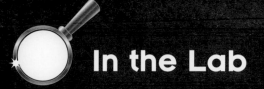

In the Lab

Cell Regulation

Osmosis is what happens when water moves from an area where there is a lot of water to an area where there is little. Imagine a dam that breaks. The water in the high area rushes toward the water in the low area. The rush does not stop until both sides are equal. Because water can pass freely in and out of a cell, there has to be an equal concentration outside the cell as inside. If not, the water outside would continue to rush into the cell until it exploded.

Jelly Belly

Inside a cell is jelly-like "stuff" called the **cytoplasm**. It is about 65 percent water.

Around the jelly is a **cytoskeleton** made of protein. The cytoskeleton is to the cell as bones are to our bodies. It's what gives a cell its strength and shape. The cytoskeleton also helps a cell move without collapsing. We used to think that only eukaryotic cells had a cytoskeleton. Yet recent studies show cytoskeletons in some bacteria, too.

A microscope shows a HeLa cell, one of a line of cancer cells being kept alive for use in research.

The **endoplasmic reticulum** (ER) is a series of tubes found in eukaryotic cells. The tubes zigzag through the cells like roads and highways. The "roads" connect the nucleus to the other organelles. The ER can be either rough or smooth. Proteins travel through the rough ER. Proteins are either sent to parts of the cell where they are needed or to the **Golgi apparatus**, where they are stored for future use. The smooth ER makes and stores compounds used for energy.

The Golgi apparatus (also called the Golgi complex) looks like a bunch of deflated balloons. Extra proteins and fats are stored here until they are sorted, packaged, and sent out. The Golgi apparatus can transfer proteins within the cell whenever and wherever they are needed.

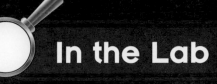

In the Lab

Science of Cooking
The outer cells of asparagus pop when plunged into boiling water, turning the vegetable a bright shade of green. If you cook asparagus too long, the cells will release acid. The vegetable will turn an ugly grey.

This model of a cell's organelles shows the structure of the Golgi apparatus.

The Power Plant

Mitochondria are sausage-shaped structures in the cytoplasm of eukaryotic cells. Mitochondria are responsible for changing food into energy. This is why they are nicknamed the "power plant." Mitochondria take sugar and other nutrients and convert them to **ATP (adenosine triphosphate)**. ATP is what gives the cell energy.

Mitochondria are perhaps the strangest of cell parts. They have their own separate genetic material. They work independently of the nucleus. They also divide independently of the cell. Scientists have a theory about this. They believe that millions of years ago, mitochondria were single prokaryotic cells living all on their own. Then, these one-celled organisms were swallowed by larger eukaryotic cells. The eukaryotic cells did not digest them. The two cells formed a cooperative relationship instead.

Mitochondria act as cells trapped within cells. The eukaryotic cell provides nutrients. The prokaryotic mitochondria convert the nutrients to ATP. The ATP provides the cell with energy.

Mitochondria have their own genetic material and divide separately from the cell.

Recycling Center

Vesicles are sacs that store or transport matter, or get rid of waste. **Lysosomes** are vesicles in eukaryotic cells that act as recycling centers. They contain **enzymes** that help the cell break down unnecessary proteins, fats, and other waste. Lysosomes are surrounded by their own membrane. This membrane protects the cell from the powerful enzymes. If the lysosomes were to break open, their enzymes could damage the cell.

White blood cells contain a large number of lysosomes. These blood cells fight disease. If their lysosomes don't work properly, serious diseases can occur.

These Rickettsia have infected a mouse with a form of typhus.

Meet Many-Times-Great-Gramps Rickettsia

Way back when mitochondria were free-living cells, they were related to Rickettsia. This is a bacteria group that is still around. It can make us sick with illnesses like typhus. We all have genetic material for Rickettsia in our bodies! So these bacteria are actually our ancestors.

At the Factory

Ribosomes are like the cell's protein factory. These tiny bead-shaped particles are found in both prokaryotic and eukaryotic cells. In eukaryotic cells, ribosomes form in the nucleus. From there, they are sent out into the cytoplasm. The nucleus sends messages to the ribosomes using **ribonucleic acid (RNA)**. The RNA tells the ribosomes which proteins the cell needs to grow. In prokaryotic cells, the ribosomes are smaller and are found throughout the cytoplasm.

Like a power plant produces energy to serve people in one area, ribosomes produce protein for the cell.

Eukaryotic plant cells also have a very large vesicle called a **vacuole**. The vacuole takes up about 50 to 95 percent of the space inside the cell. *Vacuole* means "empty space." Yet the vacuole does a lot. The vacuole presses outward against the cell wall. This helps keep a plant cell stable. It also allows the plant to grow tall. The vacuole serves as a space to store water, nutrients, and even waste. The vacuole can change its shape and size to suit the needs of the cell.

In animal cells, vacuoles have a smaller role. They can be used to transport waste. The vacuoles also hold unwanted matter. This includes bacteria that have been accidentally swallowed up by the cell.

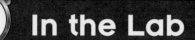

In the Lab

Molecular Post Office
Ribosomes send proteins where the cell needs them. But how do ribosomes know where to send a specific protein? Just like the zip code or postal code on an envelope, there is a signal sequence at the end of each protein. This sequence tells the ribosome the protein's destination!

These ribosomes were taken from bacteria found in feces. The photo has been colorized.

Brains of the Operation

A eukaryotic cell has a nucleus that acts as the cell's brain. The round nucleus is surrounded by a wall called the nuclear membrane or nuclear envelope. Small holes in the wall allow molecules in and out of the nucleus. Messages can pass through each of these tiny holes as quickly as 10 per second!

This image shows a human nerve cell in action.

Chromosomes are tiny beaded threads made of proteins. In eukaryotic cells they are found in the nucleus. The chromosomes are the cell's genetic material. They carry the cell's **DNA**. *DNA* is short for *deoxyribonucleic acid*. DNA is divided into smaller units called **genes**. Basically, genes decide what a cell's job in an organism will be. They also decide how a plant or an animal appears. Typical human cells have 46 chromosomes. Butterfly cells have 380!

DNA is the shape of a spiral ladder or staircase. It is about 1,000 times the length of the actual cell. It has to twist and fold into itself in order to fit inside the nucleus.

The **nucleolus** is a somewhat round spot found within the nucleus of a eukaryotic cell. It is made of protein and a kind of acid. It is the nucleolus that is responsible for sending the messages that control the cell.

In the Lab

You Are a Genius!
Human brain cells can hold five times as much information as an encyclopedia!

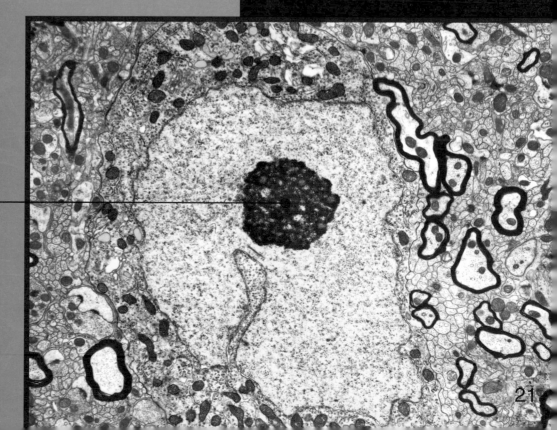

Inside the cell body of a neuron, the nucleolus is quite clear.

What's for Dinner?

Every day your body produces 300 billion new cells. Your body needs food to keep you up and running. It also needs to repair and build new cells. Just like you, cells need to eat. They need food for energy so they can move, grow, and reproduce.

Cells can use a variety of foods, including compounds such as glucose (sugar), lipids (fats), and proteins. Very tiny food molecules can enter easily through the plasma membrane. Larger food molecules have to be engulfed by the cell.

You need food for energy. Your cells need a source of energy, too.

Watch My Moves

In order to get food and oxygen, the cell must move toward what it needs. Movement is important to all cells. It is especially necessary for single-celled organisms. There are several different types of cell movement.

Single prokaryotic cells are able to move using a **flagellum**. A flagellum is made of protein. It looks like a long, skinny tail. The tail wiggles back and forth and moves the cell forward in a gliding motion.

Some eukaryotic cells move using **cilia**. Cilia are like fine hairs covering the outside of a cell. Like flagella, the cilia wiggle, moving the cell wherever it needs to go.

Other eukaryotic cells look like they're crawling. To do this, they press their cytoplasm against the cell membrane, creating a kind of "foot." The foot moves forward and then drags the rest of the cell with it.

E. coli bacteria move by using flagella, which are like tails.

Within the respiratory system, the surface has many cells with cilia.

Energize Me

After a cell takes in nutrients, it has to change that food into energy. In cells, this process is called respiration. There are two types: **aerobic respiration** and **anaerobic respiration**.

Aerobic means "with oxygen." There are many chemical stages of aerobic respiration. The first series of stages happen in the cytoplasm. The next require oxygen and happen in the mitochondria. Throughout the process, ATP (adenosine triphosphate) is produced. ATP is a cell's fuel.

Electrons are the negatively charged particles that can rub off atoms. During ATP production, electrons from the food source go into the cell. Afterward, these electrons need to be removed. This is where oxygen comes in. The elements hydrogen and oxygen combine to make water. Because water can enter and exit the cell freely, it washes the atomic junk out with it.

Exercise can be aerobic or anaerobic, depending on how your cells are activated.

Anaerobic means "without oxygen." This type of respiration happens in certain kinds of bacteria cells that cannot handle oxygen. It also happens in muscle cells of animals and people when they need a sudden burst of energy and cannot get enough oxygen for aerobic respiration to work.

Anaerobic respiration begins in the cytoplasm. The process continues in the cytoplasm with something called fermentation. During fermentation, the remaining glucose is changed into a type of acid or alcohol.

Queen bees live longer than workers. The way each kind of bee processes enzymes has a lot to do with it.

In the Lab

Bee Bouncers
Bees often eat nectar from fruit that has fermented. This nectar contains alcohol. The bees then have trouble flying. If they manage to get home and try to enter the hive, they are rejected and sometimes punished by the guard bees!

Taking Out the Trash

In eukaryotic cells, lysosomes are always breaking down unwanted matter. Sometimes worn-out mitochondria need to be destroyed and replaced. The lysosomes also digest unwanted proteins, fats, and acids. Foreign bacteria that have invaded a cell also get destroyed.

If the cell discovers that a foreign bacterium has entered, the endoplasmic reticulum (ER) surrounds the bacterium. This cuts the foreign matter off from the rest of the cell, forming a vacuole, or empty space. The lysosomes then attach themselves to the vacuole. They let their powerful enzymes go to work. The enzymes break down the unwanted material. Then the little package, a vesicle, needs to be dumped.

The vesicle is like a tiny trash bag. The cell has to get rid of it. This process is called **exocytosis**. It has steps that can seem complicated, but basically, the cell gets rid of the trash.

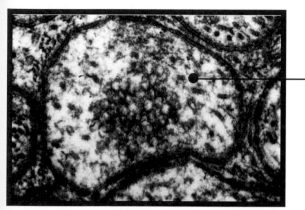

This cross section of a nerve fiber shows actual vesicles.

Killer Cells
Certain cells in your body are called T cells. They are known as natural killers. If your immune system detects unhealthy cells, it sends out the killer cells to hunt them down. Once the sick cells are located, the T cells smuggle a certain protein into them. This protein triggers the sick cell's self-destruction.
It terminates itself!

You create trash.
So do your cells.

27

Let's Split

Each cell is a living thing with its own life cycle: it grows, matures, reproduces, and dies. In multi-celled creatures, such as humans, several million cells die each day. The dead cells are constantly replaced by new ones. The life span of certain cells varies. In humans, some cells last a lifetime, while others last a few days.

So, how do we get new cells? They divide. The two asexual types of cell division are called **binary fission** and **mitosis**. Most cells divide this way.

Prokaryotic cells are organized rather simply. To reproduce, they begin by making a copy of their DNA. The original and the copy DNA attach themselves to the opposite ends of the cell membrane. The cell then pulls itself apart forming two complete cells. This process is binary fission.

Eukaryotic cells are more complicated. The nucleus must divide first, before the rest of the cell can. Mitosis is the division of the nucleus. The rest of the cell divides as a result. The cell makes a copy of its DNA. The cells then split apart. They become two cells that are like daughters.

The nucleus must divide first because the nucleus has the genetic information.

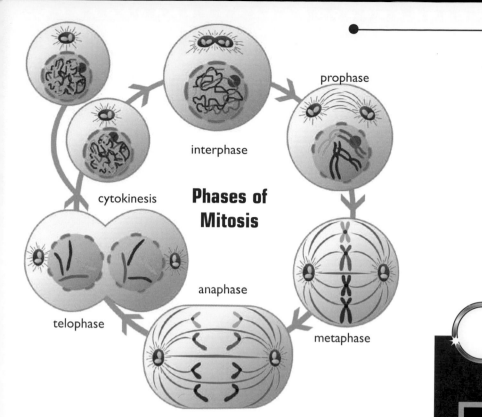

Phases of Mitosis

interphase

prophase

metaphase

anaphase

telophase

cytokinesis

These are the phases of mitosis.

1. **Prophase** DNA shortens and thickens to form chromosomes. The nuclear membrane disappears.

2. **Metaphase** Long fibers extend from the centrioles and attach themselves to the chromosomes. The chromosomes line up in the center of the cell.

3. **Anaphase** The fibers shorten and pull the chromosomes apart. The chromosomes begin to move toward opposite ends of the cell.

4. **Telophase** The chromosomes reach the opposite ends of the cell. The nuclear membrane reappears around each new nucleus. The long fibers disappear.

Next comes cytokinesis. The cell splits apart and becomes two sister cells.

In the Lab

The Terminator
To stop mitosis from getting out of control, every cell has a built-in clock that tells it when it is no longer needed. The cell terminates itself when the time is up.

Once Upon a Single Cell

Human cells have two sets of 23 chromosomes. This is a total of 46. In sex cells, however, a process called **meiosis** takes place. This produces cells that have only 23 chromosomes each. This is half the amount of other cells. In males these cells are called sperm. In females they are called eggs. When a sperm cell comes together with an egg cell, a new cell is created. The new cell has all 46 chromosomes.

Meiosis I begins as the cell starts making a copy of its DNA.

1. **Prophase I** DNA shortens and thickens to form chromosomes. Pairs of similar chromosomes line up tightly beside each other. The nuclear membrane disappears.

2. **Metaphase I** Long fibers extend from the centrioles and attach themselves to the chromosomes. The chromosomes line up in the center of the cell.

3. **Anaphase I** The fibers shorten and pull one of the matching pairs of chromosomes toward opposite ends of the cell.

4. **Telophase I** The movement is complete. Each end of the cell has 23 chromosomes. The nuclear membrane reappears around each new nucleus. The long fibers disappear.

5. **Cytokinesis** The cell splits into two cells. The chromosomes do not duplicate again.

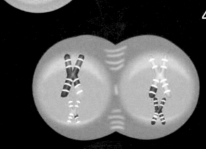

Next comes meiosis II:

6. **Prophase II** The
   nuclear membranes
   in both cells
   disappear again.

7. **Metaphase II**
   Long fibers attach
   themselves to the
   chromosomes. The
   chromosomes line
   up in the center
   of the cell.

8. **Anaphase II** The fibers
   shorten and pull the
   chromosomes apart.
   The chromosomes
   begin to move
   toward opposite
   ends of the cell.

9. **Telophase II** The
   chromosomes reach
   the opposite ends of
   the cell. The nuclear
   membrane reappears
   around each new
   nucleus. The long
   fibers disappear.

Getting the Signals

Cells are busy all the time. They convert food to energy, make protein, take out the trash, and reproduce. At a basic level, a cell is always communicating within itself. The nucleus is constantly sending information to, and receiving information from, the other parts of the cell. This system of communication is responsible for all the amazing things that happen inside a cell.

Genetics is now part of medical counseling.

Yet the cell also has the ability to communicate with other cells. It can happen in a variety of ways. A cell can communicate with another cell by coming into direct contact with it. Cells can also communicate over short or long distances.

Molecules that leave one cell and travel to another to send a message are called **hormones**. Hormones are chemical messengers between cells. The messengers affect how organs function. Cells receive the information through proteins called receptors.

Unfortunately, when messages between cells are not clear, serious diseases can happen. For example, cancer and diabetes occur because of cell miscommunication. Scientists hope they can one day jump into the conversation. They want to clear up the misunderstanding and cure these diseases.

In the Lab

Fight or Flight
Humans and animals are programmed to respond to danger in one of two ways. They either fight or they run away. If an animal is being attacked, it will need a sudden burst of energy. In preparation, nerve cells send messages to a variety of other cells telling them to release extra energy.

The fight or flight response in animals was first described in 1915.

It Makes Me Sick

Sometimes when cells divide, something goes wrong with the chromosomes. This is called **genetic mutation**. It can lead to serious diseases such as cystic fibrosis, which affects the lungs. However, not all genetic mutations are bad. Sometimes it's these changes that help an organism adapt to a new environment.

Bacteria

A bacterium is made up of one prokaryotic cell. Bacteria have many important jobs. For example, they help Earth decompose its waste. They also help us digest our food. Most of the bacteria in our bodies are harmless. However, some types of bacteria can cause diseases. Strep throat and pneumonia are caused by bacteria. Anthrax, a deadly disease in cattle which can kill humans, too, is caused by bacteria. Bacterial infections can be mild or dangerous. Antibiotics are medicines used to treat bacterial infections.

Viruses

Viruses are 20 to 100 times smaller than bacteria. They are not independent organisms. To stay alive, they must hijack living cells. They then use the parts of that cell for their own reproduction. Viruses are like the criminals of the microscopic world.

Viruses are infectious. This means they are passed from one living thing to another. People can spread viruses to other people by coughing and sneezing. Coughs travel about 60 mph (97 km/h). Coughs spray germs far and wide. Colds and flu are caused by viruses. It's no wonder people catch colds and flu so easily.

Humans are able to protect themselves from viruses in several ways. If a certain virus infects our body, our immune system kicks in and starts killing the infected cells.

In the Lab

My Computer Has the Flu
Computer viruses are small software programs that are designed to spread from one computer to another. They interfere with computer operation.

Chapter 4

Even though scientists have been studying cells for hundreds of years, they are making new and exciting discoveries all the time. What is happening in labs will affect your life.

In multi-celled organisms, cells become specialized. They take on a certain shape and become responsible for a specific job. But how does this happen when the DNA in each cell of an organism is identical?

Switch on the Future

Imagine your genes are like a string of lights. Imagine identical strings of lights are in each of your cells. Now, imagine that in one type of cell, the first two lights are turned on, and the rest are switched off. In another cell, only the first and last lights are shining. Think of all the possible combinations! Switching certain genes on and others off is what turns one cell into a muscle cell and another cell into a blood cell or a bone cell or skin cell. This is called **differentiation**.

Stem cells can be encouraged to take on the work of almost any body cell.

Red blood cells and white blood cells perform different jobs.

Stem cells are amazing cells because they are unspecialized. Stem cells are found in adult tissues or human embryos. They are like blanks. If the right genes are switched on and the right genes are switched off, stem cells can be turned into any cell in your body! This discovery is one of the most exciting discoveries of our time. Imagine the possibilities. Maybe one day, people with damaged or defective cells can have them replaced with brand-new ones. Scientists are already busy making these miracles happen. They are able to create new blood vessels from adult bone marrow stem cells. Some people who were confined to wheelchairs are even walking again because their broken bones were able to be healed with stem cells.

In the Lab

Can Monkey Teeth Cure Diseases Like Parkinson's?
As incredible as it sounds, stem cells from monkeys' teeth can stimulate growth in human brain cells.

Mirror, Mirror, in My Brain

On a hot summer day in 1995, scientists in Italy made a big discovery. They were trying to figure out which brain cells (neurons) were responsible for different movements. They had a monkey sitting in a chair. He was waiting to undergo testing. A student walked into the lab with an ice cream cone. As the student brought the ice cream up to his mouth, the monitor connected to the monkey began to beep! The scientists noticed that the cells in the monkey's brain responsible for that exact same movement began firing at the exact same time. It was as though the monkey were raising his hand to his mouth to eat the ice cream. This led to the discovery of mirror cells, or **mirror neurons**.

Mirror neurons were so-named because they let us copy actions and feelings, much like a mirror copies an image.

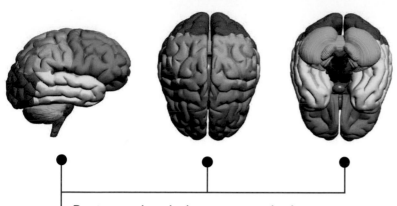

Brain studies help us map which neurons become active when and why they do.

Mirror cells in our brains allow us to copy what we see and what we hear. They even allow us to copy emotions. Do you feel sad when you watch someone else cry? That's because your mirror cells are imitating what that person is feeling. People with a lot of empathy for others have a lot of mirror cells hard at work.

Some people have a great deal of difficulty imitating others. Autism spectrum disorder is a neurological disorder. Children with autism have trouble learning to speak, making certain movements, and understanding other people's emotions. One reason is they have difficulty imitating. Although there are many factors that may cause autism, defective mirror neurons may play a role.

In the Lab

Can Playing Violent Video Games Make You Violent?
According to mirror cell research, the answer is yes. A study found that when children watched violent television, their mirror neurons were activated. This increased the chances that the children would behave violently.

It's Alive

In 1818, a 19-year-old woman named Mary Shelly wrote a novel known popularly as *Frankenstein*. Although *Frankenstein* is often classified as a horror story, it's actually a brilliant science-fiction novel. It examines the dangers and dilemmas of creating artificial life. Mary Shelly dreamed up the idea of a mad scientist creating a hideous monster by piecing together parts from dead bodies. It is safe to say that she had no clue what would be happening today.

Nearly 200 years later, scientists are hard at work creating artificial life from nothing but mere protein molecules. Scientists at Harvard University have taken a giant step forward in the creation of artificial life. They have been able to put together synthetic ribosomes. This new matter acts like the cell's protein-producing machinery. The fake ribosomes work the way natural ones do. They produce a tricky protein called *firefly luciferase*.

On a firefly, a special protein on its bottom glows in the dark.

The scientists took apart the ribosomes from bacteria called *E. coli* and then reassembled the parts. In that way, they created synthetic ribosomes. Ribosomes are one of the most complicated parts of the cell. This discovery has moved the world one huge step forward in the creation of artificial life.

What, do you think, will we be able to do with artificial life? What problems might it create? What problems might it solve?

In the Lab

Live Longer
Have scientists found the secret of youth in cells? Scientists have confirmed that anti-aging and ribosome protein production are linked to your diet. So what you have heard is true. Eat well, stay healthy, and live longer!

Genetics is a growing field of research.

Chapter 5

Your Health

You are made of cells, and your cells are alive. Here are a few tips on keeping you and those cells of yours in good shape.

Hair: Hair is made of dead cells that have hardened and pushed upward from your scalp. The only living cells in your hair are in the follicle. The protein that makes up your hair is the same protein that makes up feathers, claws, nails, and hooves. To keep your hair healthy and shiny, include brown rice and leafy green vegetables in your diet.

Skin cells: Your skin cells protect you. Make sure you protect them. Slather on the sunscreen. Wear a hat to protect your skin cells from the harmful UV rays of the Sun.

Blood cells: Are your cells getting enough vitamins? For healthy red blood cells, you need vitamin B12. You are fine if you eat meat, eggs, and dairy products regularly. Are you a vegetarian? Make sure you are getting enough vitamin B12 from some other source.

It is easier to grow healthy hair when you have a healthful diet.

Click!
Images pass through your eyes and into your brain as fast as a flickering light. So how is your brain able to grasp anything? According to scientists, your brain cells have a memory. It is as if the cells take a photo of what they see and are able to store it for about two whole seconds.

Your brain cells need exercise, just as your muscle cells do.

Bone cells: Bones are alive. They are made of living cells that help them grow and mend themselves. Exercise helps our bones by stimulating new cell growth. Getting enough calcium is also important.

Brain cells: You exercise your body, but do you exercise your brain? Keep your brain cells healthy by keeping them active. Activity in a brain builds connections and even generates new brain cells. Pick up a good book and give your brain a workout.

Make Your Own Edible Cell

Materials:

- Medium-sized bowl
- 2–3 packages flavored gelatin (such as Jell-O)
- 1 large gumball or jawbreaker for the nucleus
- Variety of candies, gummies, and sprinkles

Method:

1. Make the gelatin according to the instructions (use slightly less water).
2. Place the gelatin in the bowl and refrigerate until it begins to thicken.
3. Add various candies, gummies, gumballs, and sprinkles.
4. Return to the refrigerator for several hours or overnight.
5. When firm, loosen the gelatin by placing the bowl into warm water for several minutes (being careful not to submerge the bowl).
6. Cover the bowl with a large plate and flip! You have made your very own edible cell!

For Further Information

Books

Allman, Toney. **Great Medical Discoveries: Stem Cells**. Farmington Hills, Mich.: Lucent Books, 2006.

Sherman, Josepha. **How Do We Know the Nature of the Cell.** (Great Scientific Questions and the Scientists Who Answered Them) New York: Rosen Publishing Group Inc., New York, 2005.

Snedden, Robert. **Cells & Life: The World of the Cell: Life on a Small Scale**. Chicago: Heinemann Library, 2003.

Web sites

www.cellsalive.com/

www.icnet.uk/kids/cellsrus/page4.html

www.biologyinmotion.com/atp/

← DNA

quote

"Any living cell carries with it the experience of a billion years of experimentation by its ancestors."
Max Delbrück
(1906–1981, German-American biophysicist)

Glossary

adenosine triphosphate (ATP) A high-energy molecule that fuels the cell

aerobic respiration Release of energy that requires oxygen

anaerobic respiration Release of energy that does not require oxygen

archaea Single-celled prokaryotic organisms that are not bacteria

atoms Fundamental particles that make up living and nonliving things

bacteria Single-celled prokaryotic organisms that are not archaea

binary fission A type of cell division in prokaryotic cells

chromosomes Coiled threads of DNA containing genes

cilia Tiny tail-like or hairy structures providing movement on some cells

compound microscope A microscope with more than one lens

cytoplasm The jelly-like substance inside a cell

cytoskeleton The cell's skeleton

deoxyribonucleic acid (DNA) Long strand of genetic information found in the cell's nucleus

differentiation Process in which a cell becomes more specialized

electrons Charged particles within atoms

endoplasmic reticulum (ER) A series of canals, like veins, running through the cell

enzymes Proteins that help speed up specific chemical reactions

eukaryotic cells Plant or animal cells with a nucleus

exocytosis Process in which a cell ejects waste

flagellum A long, thin structure providing movement on some cells

genes Sections of a chromosome that code for a certain protein

genetic mutation When chromosomes go wrong during cell division

Golgi apparatus Part of a cell mainly devoted to creating proteins

hormones Chemicals that act like messenger molecules in the body

lysosomes Parts of cells containing digestive enzymes

meiosis Type of cell division which forms sex cells

mirror neurons Nerve cells that work when animals act or see the same act

mitochondria Part of the cell that converts nutrients into energy

mitosis Type of cell division that forms two identical cells

molecules Smallest unit of a substance

multicellular Made up of more than one cell

nucleoid Large space inside prokaryotic cells that contains genetic material

nucleolus Structure made of protein and nucleic acid located inside the nucleus

nucleus Control center of plant or animal cells

organelles General name for parts of a cell

osmosis Movement of water molecules through a membrane so concentrations will be equal on both sides of the membrane

plasma membrane Structure that regulates what goes in and out of a cell

prokaryotic cells Cells that do not have a nucleus

proteins Large molecules needed for the structure and function of a body's cells

ribonucleic acid (RNA) Molecule that takes genetic information from the nucleus to the ribosomes

ribosomes Parts of the cell that build proteins

stem cells Cells that can become many kinds of cells

unicellular organisms One-celled living things

vacuole Space in a cell that stores food and nutrients

vesicles Small sacs that store or transport substances

Index